MM.LAFLEUR

NEW YORK

MM.LaFleur's

WEAR

A guide to building
your ultimate professional uniform.

TO

By Tory Hoen & Sarah LaFleur

WORK

A new dress doesn't get you anywhere.
It's the life you're living in the dress,
and the sort of life you had lived before,
and what you will do in it later.

Diana Vreeland

INTRODUCTION

Hey, you.
Yes, you—
with the job.

Getting dressed for work should be fun, or at the very least, it should be easy. But today's professional woman faces a unique conundrum. She's inundated with fashion inspiration (style blogs, glossy magazines, runway images), but still left without much guidance when it comes to dressing for the office—you know, the place where she spends most of her waking hours.

CHALLENGE #1

There's a fundamental disconnect between what the fashion industry is selling, and what professional women actually need. We love poring over the pages of *Vogue*, but when it comes down to it, few of the looks therein actually translate to the professional world; and most fashion blogs do very little to illuminate the (often unspoken) codes of dressing for work. Have you ever showed up to a formal client meeting in a romper? How'd that go?

CHALLENGE #2

Many dedicated workwear brands are failing to keep up with the discerning tastes of the women they serve. Their offerings are overly stiff, drab, or poorly made; and those who wear them feel the need to run home and change into "real" clothes before going out after work.

CHALLENGE #3

Dressing for work is a nuanced proposition, and while women don't need instructions on what to wear, many of us would like some advice. Some companies have learned the hard way that this advice should not come from elderly male senior partners, whose attempts to "guide" women come off as condescending and out of touch. A more objective resource would be nice, which brings us to... this book!

We wrote this guide for all women of purpose—women who have #BetterThingsToDo than agonize in front of the closet each morning. Like you, we know how hard it can be to shop for work and to balance personal style with the sartorial expectations of the workplace.

But can we let you in on a secret? It doesn't have to be so hard. In fact, it should be a pleasure to develop and pursue your own weekday style. So let's create a new paradigm for how professional women think about their clothes. After all, your professional style *is* your style. Embrace it, love it, and by all means, work it!

In these pages, we give you a no-nonsense four-step system for cultivating a career-making wardrobe.

In *Step 1*, you'll envision and define your perfect closet.

In *Step 2*, we'll help you make sense of your current work wardrobe and make room for new office-ready pieces.

In *Step 3*, we'll make a concrete plan for filling up your hangers based on what you need and how much you want to spend.

In *Step 4*, we'll divulge our favorite brands and go-to items, and we'll coach you on how to assess quality and make savvy shopping decisions.

From there, we'll steer you around potential *On the Job* pitfalls. And for those of you just entering the workforce, our *First Job Checklist* will help you prep with confidence.

By the time you put this book down, you'll know exactly how to build and maintain your ultimate work wardrobe—and you'll be excited about the process. We promise.

But first, let's get philosophical.

PHILOSOPHY: CREATE YOUR UNIFORM

*In which you'll learn to dress like
Karl Lagerfeld—sort of.*

Get dressed like you're the president (no matter what your politics).

In a *Vanity Fair* article by Michael Lewis, Barack Obama said: "You'll see I wear only gray or blue suits. I'm trying to pare down decisions. I don't want to make decisions about what I'm eating or wearing. Because I have too many other decisions to make."

You might not be the president (yet), but that doesn't mean you shouldn't dress with POTUS-like efficiency.

Of course, men have it easy: Gray or navy suit? Blue or red tie? There are only so many combinations to consider. They have a uniform, and they stick to it. In many cases, this uniform has been passed down from generation to generation, with fathers teaching their sons everything from ideal pant length to tie-tying tricks.

Women face a much more nuanced sartorial puzzle. In many industries, there is no clear precedent for how we should dress. And while our array of options might feel like freedom of choice, it's actually a recipe for ongoing confusion and early-morning angst.

Our solution? Look like a lady, but dress like a dude.

In other words: Get a uniform.

A uniform? That sounds oppressive!

Fair point. Back in '70s and '80s when women were fighting to get a foothold in the corporate world, many of them adopted what was the equivalent of a feminized men's suit. This is not what we're advocating when we say you should create your own uniform; nor are we suggesting that you break out the old prep-school kilt.

An effective uniform is merely a means of streamlining your many options and refining your style story, and there's scientific evidence that explains why this is a smart strategy.

Have you heard of the chocolate experiment? In 2000, psychologists Sheena Iyengar and Mark Lepper randomized individuals into two groups: The first could choose from six types of chocolate, while the second could choose from 30. In the end, those with 30 choices ended up being less satisfied with their decisions than those who only had six options. Whether it's chocolate or pencil skirts, too much choice leads to stress.

Everyone's doing it.

Many of the world's most celebrated professionals have adopted a uniform of sorts. Sheryl Sandberg, Hillary Clinton, and Christine Lagarde all opt for elegant, streamlined looks. And even some of fashion's most powerful figures—people who could wear anything—elect to keep their looks consistent. Karl Lagerfeld always wears a black suit with a white shirt, black tie, and his infamous sunglasses. Anna Wintour is most often seen in a prim shift dress accented with a classic cardigan or jacket.

These folks don't dress this way by chance. Like Obama, they dress this way to minimize decision-making so they can actually get to work.

Shop with your head, not with your heart.

We know, we know. It sounds cold and inhumane, but trust us, your life will be immeasurably easier if you have a closetful of useful items, rather than drawers full of never-worn "going-out tops."

In this guide, we'll help you pinpoint exactly what you need to succeed. No more, no less. The cardinal rule in building your uniform is clear-headed, laser-focused, hyper-calculated decision-making. Learn to plan ahead; do not buy on impulse or at the last-minute.

But the heart wants what it wants!

Indeed it does. So let's compromise: You can indulge your heart when you shop for weekend clothes—just not when you're shopping for work.

Let's get started.

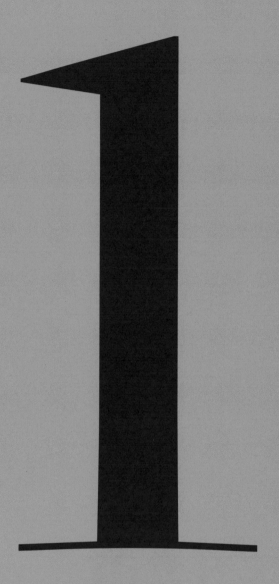

STEP 1

—

ENVISION YOUR PERFECT WARDROBE

*In which you'll choose your professional
spirit animal—and more.*

It's time to show your closet who's boss.

"I have nothing to wear."

Can we please do away with this phrase, once and for all? As women, we utter these words way too often, when what we really mean is: *"I have nothing I want to wear."* When it comes to dressing for work, the feeling grows exponentially, as does the angst that goes along with it.

Don't waste another minute feeling this way. Instead, resolve to eliminate stress by simplifying and streamlining your decision-making process, just like Anna, Karl, Elizabeth, and Steve.

The first step is to envision a closet that has everything you need, and nothing you don't.

Find your professional spirit animal.

Yes, you'll need to be clear-eyed and decisive in order to create the perfect work wardrobe. But even so, there is room to be yourself and carve out your own professional persona.

DO
THIS

Create a Mood Board!

Before you edit your closet or even think about going shopping, let your imagination run a little wild. Bust out the glue stick and create a workwear mood board that taps into your professional personality and look (or create a digital version on Pinterest or Tumblr).

As you collect ideas, notice which images inspire you: Claire Underwood? Olivia Pope? A wild-eyed fox? An M.C. Escher graphic pattern? Sounds good.

Tip — For more inspiration targeted to your body type, check out the book *The Science of Sexy* by Bradley Bayou.

Describing your style.

DO THIS

Now that you've matched some images to the vision, find a few words and concepts that reflect how you want to look and feel at work. Without over-thinking it, circle the words below that most appeal to your professional sensibility.

Black	*Gray*	*White*
Pink	*Red*	*Orange*
Colorful	*Muted*	*Neutral*
Patterned	*Tailored*	*Curvy*
Loose	*Fitted*	*Comfortable*
Pretty	*Sexy*	*Powerful*
Cozy	*Effortless*	*Cool*
Elegant	*Trendy*	*Creative*
Exotic	*Basic*	*Intricate*

Beige	*Navy*	*Brown*
Green	*Purple*	*Blue*
Dark	*Bright*	*Floral*
A-line	*Straight-leg*	*Structured*
Sharp	*Polished*	*Preppy*
Strong	*Easy*	*Relaxed*
Modern	*Classic*	*Traditional*
Luxurious	*Romantic*	*Edgy*
Simple	*Complex*	*Hand-crafted*

So, which words did you choose?

Keep them in mind as you build your new work wardrobe.

STEP 2

—

ORGANIZE & EDIT

In which you'll tame the beast that
is your current closet.

Think like an editor. Break out the red pen.

Best-selling author Stephen King often touts the famous mantra: "Kill your darlings."

What he means is: Don't get sentimental about things that don't serve your greater purpose. For the writer, that's a sentence (or a page, or a chapter) that doesn't enhance the larger narrative. For the working woman, it's those clothes that you're attached to, but that you never actually wear.

When it comes to your professional wardrobe, there's a fine balance. You need to have enough clothes to meet the demands of your lifestyle; but if you have too many options, you'll get lost in them. Below, we present three tried-and-true rules to help you edit like a pro.

1. Separate Work & Play

Your first mission: Separate your "play" clothes from your "work" clothes. You might think you own a lot of cross-over items, but you'll be surprised by how few things genuinely make sense for both work and fancy-free frolicking.

Once you've decided what is workwear versus leisurewear (we love that word), create dedicated space for each. If you can swing two separate closets, we're impressed. If not, just divide your closet in two, and be rigorous about storing clothes on their designated sides. Tailored pencil skirts should not fraternize with leather hot pants!

2. Be Ruthless

You have room to be a bit sentimental, but you must also learn to edit decisively. A few cherished pieces may last a lifetime, but that wine-stained blouse must go, no matter how many memorable nights you've had in it.

Remember the mood board you created? And the word cloud? Adhere to that vision as you make the tough decisions. If you're going for a sleek, sophisticated wardrobe, it's probably time to bid adieu to anything overly frilly, ruffled, or sequined.

3. Expire & Retire

Most of us know that food has an expiration date. We are quick to upgrade our smartphones. So why do we have such a hard time saying goodbye to past-their-prime clothes?

Like much of what we own, clothes have a shelf life. Buy them with thought, handle them with care, and make repairs when necessary. But accept the fact that they will have to be retired one day.

Dry-cleaners and tailors can work wonders to resuscitate a piece, but don't hang on to anything that is:

×   Permanently stained

×   Ripped beyond repair

×   Missing crucial buttons that you can't replace

×   Perpetually wrinkled or messy-looking

×   Threadbare or frayed

To keep or to toss?
If you still can't decide, ask yourself:

1 — Have you worn it in the past year?

YES? Keep it!

NO? Kick it to the curb.

2 — Whether or not you consider yourself to be an adult, decide:
"Is this something an adult would wear?"

YES? Keep it!

NO? See ya!

Time to make a list.

It sounds dorky (okay, it is dorky), but taking a detailed inventory of what's in your closet is the best way to keep track of your evolving wardrobe. That way, you can figure out what you're working with each morning, notice any gaps, and keep track of items that have fallen out of rotation or need replacing.

DO
THIS

Using the chart on pages 36 and 37, start by writing down every item in your closet that you deem "work appropriate." Next, see how many outfits you can make from these items. (You'll map them out on pages 38 and 39.)

× If you're at ten, bravo! You're done. You probably don't need to go shopping for work clothes. (Why do we say ten? We'll explain on page 51.)

× If you're at fewer than ten, don't fret. In the following chapters, we'll help you figure out how to fill the holes until you have a complete—and super snazzy—wardrobe.

Tip — **You can also use an app called Closet+ (*closetapp.com*) to keep an inventory of your clothes, figure out how much value you're getting from each piece, and plan outfits according to your schedule.**

My current work wardrobe.

	Style	Color	Brand
Tops			
Skirts			
Dresses			
Pants			

	Style	*Color*	*Brand*
Blazers			
Knits			
Shoes			
Accessories			

How many outfits can you make?

	Dress, Skirt or Pants	Top or Blouse	Knit or Jacket	Shoes
Outfit 1				
Outfit 2				
Outfit 3				
Outfit 4				
Outfit 5				

	Dress, Skirt or Pants	Top or Blouse	Knit or Jacket	Shoes
Outfit 6				
Outfit 7				
Outfit 8				
Outfit 9				
Outfit 10				

Don't worry if you can't create ten work outfits yet. We'll get there!

STEP 3

—

PLAN
& BUDGET

In which you'll glimpse your
fashion future.

Now that you've taken stock of what's in your closet, it's time to make a plan. The success of your work wardrobe ultimately hinges on three key factors: vision, time, and money.

You've got the vision (check that mood board!). Now, do you have realistic expectations about the time it will take to realize this vision? Are you investing wisely and strategically to achieve it? Once you can answer "yes" to these questions, you'll be well on your way.

Slow and steady wins the race.

Rome was not built in a day—and neither was the ultimate work wardrobe. Though it might seem fun, going on a single no-holds-barred shopping spree is no way to outfit yourself for a career. Put your credit card on temporary lockdown and take some time to strategize. Your style evolution is a marathon, not a sprint. Plan accordingly if you want to go the distance.

Keep in mind that you are not merely acquiring clothes; you are forming smart shopping habits. Individual pieces will come and go, but if you learn to make savvy choices, your wardrobe will always reflect and enable the lifestyle you want.

The goal is to someday gaze into your closet and say $\rightarrow$

"I could happily wear everything in here."

But, let's not get ahead of ourselves.

First things first: How do I budget for clothes?

Just as you set aside money for rent or entertainment every month, create a clothing budget that will help you make conscious decisions about what to buy. You don't have to blow your savings to create a wardrobe that makes you feel like a boss. You simply have to invest wisely and build thoughtfully.

As a general rule, plan to spend 5-10% of your monthly take-home income on clothes. What's your take-home income? The part of your salary that actually ends up in your bank account after taxes, retirement savings (401k, IRA), and any other deductions.

Here's how that might pan out at different phases of your career.

 ### If you just graduated from college...

Remember the list you compiled of your current wardrobe? If you've never worked (or never worked in the environment you'll soon be working in), that list probably contained only a few work-appropriate items. As your start date approaches, the "I have nothing to wear" feeling will set in.

Don't despair—everyone feels this way. Breathe, strategize, prioritize. Don't buy things just because they're cheap, and don't buy party or weekend clothes right now. You'll soon spend 70% of your waking hours at your job, so focus your attention (and your money) on this area of your life.

Break it down: Put aside $1,000 to get yourself started (use savings, get a freelance gig, or borrow from someone who's willing to spot you). Do not buy cheap stuff—stay away from low-quality fast fashion. Instead, focus: Buy five quality outfits. These might consist of three good dresses ($450), three basic knits ($250), and two pairs of office-appropriate shoes ($300). These items will get you through your first two months on the job.

Fiscal outlook: If your take-home is $2500/month, put aside $125-$250 each month for workwear. Shop seasonally, rather than every month, so you'll have $375-$750 to spend per season. Not bad! And if you don't use up all $750, keep it on hand for when you stumble upon that too-amazing-to-pass-up item. Better yet: Invest it, and watch your fashion fund grow over time.

If you are returning to the workforce after grad school...

Depending on whether you're changing industries now that you have a graduate degree, you might not need to do much shopping—or you may have to start from scratch.

First, check yourself out—and be honest. Are you the same size you were before graduate school? If not, it's no big deal—just resist the urge to squeeze into an old pair of pants that no longer fit. Say goodbye to your favorite work cardigan if you're swimming in it. The last thing you want is to feel uncomfortable or frumpy when you start your new gig.

Then, do a careful inspection of all your pieces before you decide whether to wear, repair, or toss them. Check for moth holes, pills, and tired fabrics. Finally, consider organizing a "workwear swap" with your classmates. Some of you are switching industries, and what you wore to your last job is no longer appropriate for your new one. In these cases, one professional woman's trash is another professional woman's treasure.

Fiscal outlook: Stick to spending 5-10% of your monthly income on clothes. As you earn more, that percentage should move closer to 5%.

If you get a raise...

High five! As far as your wardrobe goes, it's time to live a little. Buy that piece you've been eyeing, and forever associate it with the fact that you rule. Then, reassess your clothing budget and proceed responsibly. You might be richer, but you should still be strategic about how you spend.

Fiscal outlook: Just because you're earning more money doesn't mean you need to spend more on clothes. Rather, consider how you're allocating your clothing budget. If you've already got a solid foundation for your wardrobe, now might be a time to spend more on statement pieces or high-quality accessories.

Create a Budget!

Monthly Take-home (after taxes,
retirement savings, and any other savings) =

....

5-10% of Monthly Take-home =

....

Seasonal Budget (5-10% of monthly take-home × 3 months) =

....

Pieces to prioritize this season:

....
....
....
....
....

Pieces to prioritize next season:

....
....
....
....
....

STEP 4

—

INVEST
& BUILD

In which you'll learn how
to shop with purpose.

Part 1:
What to Buy

Now that your funds are in order, let's get down to business! And by business, we mean shopping.

Build your "Perfect Ten."

When it comes to the breakdown of a wardrobe, every professional woman's needs are slightly different. For the purposes of this book, we're advising those who need to dress for business-casual to business-formal environments (finance, law, consulting, politics, etc.). But no matter what industry you work in, you can follow this advice. And no matter who you are, you really only need ten outfits. We've spent years testing out this theory, and we can say with supreme confidence: *Ten is the magic number.*

These outfits will look different from closet to closet. Ten dresses could be ten outfits. Five tops and two skirts could create ten outfits. Four dresses and two blazers could create ten outfits.

But no matter how many individual items you're working with, you need to be able to create ten distinct looks. If you have two pink shirts and two pairs of black pants, that really only adds up to one look (pink top, black bottom). Whereas if you have a white shirt, a pink shirt, black pants, and gray pants, that's four looks.

Remember: A uniform is not an excuse to get lazy and wear the same thing every day. It's a guideline to help you establish a consistent style.

So, are you ready to create your *Perfect Ten*?

TIP — As you're building the foundation of your work wardrobe, we strongly recommend starting with neutral colors before adding brights, patterns, and prints. That means black, gray, navy, ivory, beige, and olive. And yes, some consider a moderate splash of leopard to be a neutral.

Once you've got a healthy rotation of staples, start adding statement pieces. Just remember: Every addition needs to contribute to your *Perfect Ten*, meaning it should complement the foundation you've built. If you can't envision exactly how you'd wear a new item with your existing clothes, save yourself the trouble: Don't buy it.

The 40-40-20 Wardrobe.

Not every workday is created equal. On days when you're deskbound, a simple skirt and cozy cardigan will do. On days when you're presenting to your company's investors, you need a serious power outfit.

In addition to making sure you have ten solid outfits in your closet, think about creating a balanced wardrobe made up of *Everyday, Elevated,* and *Showstopper* pieces. If we're talking percentages, then 40-40-20 is the right balance of each.

EVERYDAY

These are the items that get you through the average workday: casual sweaters, easy dresses. They're comfortable, versatile, and perhaps even machine-washable. They look neat, but their shelf life is limited to one-two years. Yes, just like food, clothes have a shelf life—and that's okay.

 Percentage of wardrobe: 40%   *Shelf life: 1-2 years*

ELEVATED

These are high-quality pieces that form the basis of your wardrobe on days when you need to look spot-on. They might be three-season pieces like a great blazer or a tailored pencil skirt.

 Percentage of wardrobe: 40%   *Shelf life: 3-5 years*

SHOWSTOPPER

These are the pieces that you pull out for the big meeting or the speaking gig where you'll be on stage. They inspire compliments every time you wear them, and because you've invested in quality, they'll last for years.

 Percentage of wardrobe: 20%   *Shelf life: 5+ years*

DO
THIS

Time to make your shopping list!

First, review the outfit list you created on page 38.

Now, create a shopping list. While you work, consider:

× If the goal is to create your *Perfect Ten*, where are the holes in your current closet? What items do you need to create the right balance of Everyday vs. Signature vs. Power outfits?

× How many of these outfits could be *Renaissance outfits*? Renaissance outfits are versatile enough to go from a business meeting to a power lunch to a cocktail event without missing a beat. They are the professional woman's greatest weapon.

Items I still need to create my Perfect Ten.

	Style	Color	Brand
Tops			
Skirts			
Dresses			
Knits			
Blazers			
Pants			
Shoes			

Where to invest (and where to fake it).

When you're first building your work wardrobe, it's all about prioritizing. There's a commonly held myth that you should splurge on bags and shoes and skimp on the rest of your wardrobe. We beg to differ.

A pair of $700 stilettos is not going to make your workday any easier; but having an array of high-quality pieces in neutral colors will definitely simplify your life.

Invest ($200+)

Black day-to-night dress
Versatile blazer
Tailored pants or skirt
Elegant (but not flashy) bag

Spend Moderately ($50-$200)

Knits
Pencil skirt
Silk blouse
Shoes (that you can walk in!)

See What You Can Get Away With (Under $50)

Tank tops
Camisoles
T-shirts
Tights
Accessories / statement pieces that you might get tired of

Next-level statement pieces.

Once you have your core wardrobe and basic accessories, it's time to get a little bit audacious. There are certain items that will instantly elevate your look from appropriate to fabulous. Among professional women, it's understood that these pieces represent serious style added without detracting from your professionalism—and you don't have to wait until you make your first million to buy them.

1. Printed pumps.

A subtle reptile print or colorful pattern can make an otherwise neutral outfit look totally fresh.

2. A coat with a point of view.

Look for a beautifully tailored coat with a dominant design detail (a dramatic collar, a belted waist) or an unexpected color (aubergine, forest green).

3. A fur cowl, collar, or stole.

A subtle hint of fur (or faux fur!) will make any outfit feel instantly glamorous.

4. A classic watch.

Round or square, inherited or self-gifted, a beautiful watch will make you feel "done," even if it's the only accessory you wear.

5. A sassy blazer.

Keep the cut professional, but play with a subtle pattern or an atypical fabric. What's sleeker than an ivory linen blazer for summer? Nothing, that's what.

6. A luxurious scarf.

One of those silk Hermès numbers can make you look mega-classy, even when you're in jeans and a t-shirt. (Discount retailers like Century 21 and Gilt frequently have these on sale.)

Part 2: Assess Your Options

It's almost time to hit the stores, but before you storm the gates, make sure you have your priorities straight.

Treat your wardrobe like an asset.

You wouldn't invest in a car, a home, or a mutual fund without giving it serious thought. Apply this same rigor when building your wardrobe.

Whether you're buying a camisole or a cashmere coat, take a moment to assess how it fits in with what you already own. Will it strengthen your overall "portfolio" in the long run? Or are you giving in to a fleeting trend or momentary impulse?

Invest in quality. Wait, what is quality?

Don't just shop for style. A piece should move well and make you feel polished, but it should also have integrity—yes, integrity—in and of itself. So how do you really judge quality? We've got it down to a science.

Here's what to look for:

HEMS & SEAMS

× Hems and seams should be straight and clean with no puckering or bunching around the stitches.

× If it has a fragile fabric or there are areas of heavy use (pockets, zipper), a quality piece will include reinforcements like facing, lining, and binding in those areas.

× If the garment has a pattern or stripe, it should intentionally align at the seam.

× If there are pockets, they should be real and accessible (rather than just illusion pockets).

STITCHING

- × Stitches should have a consistent, even length.

- × They should be taut, but shouldn't pull the fabric or cause it to pucker.

- × Stitch lines should be clean and even, with no doubling back or loose threads.

- × A higher density of stitches usually means the garment will be sturdier.

- × Look for individual stitch length; shorter stitches tend to be stronger and less likely to break.

HAND FEEL

- × Scrunch up the fabric in your hand to get a feel for its weight, texture, and how it moves.

- × To judge how a garment will feel on your body, rub it on the inside of your wrist (a particularly sensitive area).

- × Your fingertips are intuitive and will indicate how a garment will feel against your skin all day. They'll also help you understand whether a garment has structure, is durable, or will wrinkle.

BREATHABILITY

- × Fact: Humans sweat. In order for you to stay cool and comfortable in your clothes, they need to breathe.

- × Natural fibers (wool, cotton) usually breathe well, but they can wear out sooner than synthetic fibers. High-quality synthetic fibers tend to stay fresh-looking for longer.

- × The days of "polyester = bad" are over, and some of the most comfortable and breathable fabrics are synthetics.

- × It's often smart to choose a blend of a natural fiber with a percentage of nylon or polyester, which help garments hold their shape and go the distance.

- × Be on the look-out for a brand's "signature fabric." There's a reason they use it season after season: Customers keep coming back for it.

LINING

× There's a misconception that lined garments are good quality and unlined garments are cheap. This is not always the case.

× Depending on stretch and weight, some fabrics look and feel best without lining; others (like those with intricate seams or textured fabrics) require it.

× When lining is used, check to make sure that it complements the weight, stretch, and drape of the outer layer. The lining should never be visible or shift around within the garment.

STRETCH

× We're fans of fabrics that contain stretch, because it means the garment will move with your body. To see if a garment has stretch, check the label. If it says "EA" (Elastane /Lycra /Spandex) or "PA" (Polyamide /Nylon), there's a good chance the fabric will stretch well.

× If the fabric has stretch, pull it for half a second to see how it recovers. A quick and thorough recovery means it will last longer and hold its shape throughout the day. If it doesn't snap back immediately after you release it, the garment may leave you with diaper-butt by noon. Not a great look.

Quality Calibrator

As you know by now, quality is a complex subject. Not only does it describe how a garment looks, fits and feels—it also indicates how long it will last. Don't judge a dress by its price. Do the math to figure out its long-term value.

	Retail Price	Life Span	Price per Wear
Fast-fashion Dress	$49	3 wears	$16.33
Lower-end Contemporary Brand Dress	$99	12 wears	$8.25
High-end Contemporary Brand Dress	$250	50 wears	$5 ✓
Luxury Brand Dress	$1,135	75 wears	$15.13

Don't worry about size; worry about fit.

When it comes to size, the principle of "separate work and play" continues to apply. You have two clothing sizes: your size for play clothes and your size for work clothes. Don't assume the two will be the same, especially if you like your weekend clothes to be body-hugging or oversized.

Remember: Size is just a number. It's also a fairly arbitrary (and often inconsistent) number. You may be an 8 or a "Medium" in one brand and a 12 or a "Large" in another, so it makes more sense to focus on fit.

Regardless of how you like to dress on your own time, there is a Goldilocks-like code for workwear: not too loose, not too tight, but just right. So how do you know what's "just right"? Use these tests for a work-friendly fit:

1. The VPL (Visible Panty Line) Test

Wear bikini underwear (not a thong!), and try on your outfit. Turn your back to the mirror. Move your hips, bend over, twerk if you must. If you can see your underwear lines, your outfit is too tight.

2. The Bow Test

Wear your normal work bra. Stand in front of a mirror and bow deeply. When you reach a 90° angle, look up at the mirror while holding your bow. If you can see your cleavage or any part of your bra, the cut of your top is too low.

3. The Taxi Test

Simulate stepping into a cab by lifting your leg. Can you manage to lift it comfortably without stressing any seams? If not, your outfit is too tight, and more importantly, impractical. You're a woman on the go! Make sure you can move in your clothes.

When it comes to buying work clothes, they should fit perfectly or be a tiny bit loose—you can always have things taken in.

Hey there, tailor.

Back in the day, you might have hired Coco Chanel or Elsa Schiaparelli to customize your clothes. Nowadays, it's a ready-to-wear world, but that doesn't mean you shouldn't put your local tailor to work.

Some people have a knack for finding their size right off the rack, but depending on your proportions, getting a perfect fit can be tricky. This is what tailors are for. There's nothing wrong with buying a dress that's slightly too big in a certain area (bust, hips, length) and having it taken in so it fits you to a T. If you're between sizes, always opt for the larger size.

Remember: When it comes to looking chic and confident, fit is everything. There's no need to compromise, no matter what your size.

Part 3:
Where to Buy

The longer you work, the more you'll realize: Not all workwear is created equal. Two black dresses might look identical, but spend a day in them, and you'll know instantly which has the superior design.

If you can identify the brands and products you love early on in your career, you'll know exactly where to go when you need to replace an item or update your wardrobe.

Here are a few beloved brands and go-to products that have earned a cult following for good reason.

Clothing

	$	$$	$$$
Dresses & Skirts	ANN TAYLOR ZARA	CLUB MONACO J.CREW MM.LAFLEUR	DVF ELIE TAHARI THEORY
Pants	ANN TAYLOR ZARA	BANANA REPUBLIC J.CREW MM.LAFLEUR	ALICE & OLIVIA JOSEPH THEORY
Blouses & Tops	EVERLANE ZARA	CLUB MONACO MM.LAFLEUR	DVF EQUIPMENT KATE SPADE THEORY TORY BURCH
Knits & Jackets	BODEN ZARA	J.CREW MM.LAFLEUR	ELIE TAHARI THEORY VINCE

Accessories

	$	$$	$$$
Shoes	BANANA REPUBLIC BODEN ANN TAYLOR EVERLANE	COLE HAAN M.GEMI L.K.BENNETT J.CREW STUART WEITZMAN	JIMMY CHOO NICHOLAS KIRKWOOD
Tights & Socks	LAND'S END	COMMANDO CLUB MONACO SPANX DONNA KARAN	WOLFORD
Lingerie	GAP BODY CALVIN KLEIN UNIQLO	JOURNELLE THIRDLOVE HANKY PANKY	COSABELLA NATORI CHANTELLE INTIMISSI

Anh Sundstrom

When it comes to great office style, we're always inspired by blogger Anh Sundstrom of *9 to 5 Chic* (*9to5chic.com*). Here, she divulges the pieces that anchor her work wardrobe.

My all-time best buys.

1. A black blazer.

"Nothing ties it all together like a blazer. It's also the perfect piece to take your outfit from casual to business-casual. And it doesn't hurt to leave one at the office for those meetings that pop up out of nowhere."

2. A navy sheath dress.

"Navy is a classic color, which makes it a perfect match for the classic sheath. I can dress it up or down, layer over or under, or wear as is. A sheath dress should fit perfectly—not too tight and not too loose—and it should hit right above the knee."

3. Black pumps.

"I'm a fan of single-sole, pointed-toe pumps, and I wear them constantly! The key is to find a heel height that works for you. I have 4-inch heels for my power days, and 3-inch heels for days when I'll be doing more walking."

Abra Belke

For professional style advice, the ladies of Washington D.C. look to blogger Abra Belke (a.k.a. Belle) from *Capitol Hill Style* (*caphillstyle.com*). Here, she dishes on the pieces she wears again and again.

My all-time best buys.

1. A Malene Birger reverse-leopard-print scarf.

"I actually picked this piece up on eBay. It adds a bold accent, and I wear it with all of my black separates during the colder months."

2. My black Akiko dress from MM.LaFleur.

"I bought this dress to wear to the office, but I find myself wearing it everywhere. I've added a sequin belt for cocktail parties; I've worn it with rolled sleeves and a stack of bracelets; and I pair it with red flats for conferences when I don't want to wear heels."

3. Pops of color.

"When I'm stressed and haven't slept well, I like to wear bright colors as a pick-me-up. My bright-pink pencil skirt from L.K. Bennett and my yellow blazer from Nanette Lepore are my go-to pieces for days when I need my wardrobe to convey brightness and liveliness."

A lingerie expert weighs in on underpinnings for the office.

Every great work outfit is built on a solid (and perhaps saucy) foundation. **Claire Chambers**, founder of Journelle, shares her tips on how to choose siren-worthy lingerie that will do its job while you do yours.

How do you make sure your lingerie is undetectable in the office?

Look for bras that are seamless, smooth, and have an impeccable fit. For bottoms, go for a barely-there thong like Girl Thong from Commando. When selecting solution-based lingerie, always make sure your decision is based on fit and comfort.

What are the first three pieces of lingerie every working woman should buy?

1. A well-fitting t-shirt bra. It creates a flattering silhouette under everything from a silk blouse to a cashmere sweater. And for the weekend, it looks great in its natural habitat: beneath a favorite t-shirt.

2. A seamless, comfortable bottom is key to getting through the day. I love Cosabella's Trenta in both the thong and the brief. It's lightweight, lace, and totally seamless, and it works perfectly beneath jeans, trousers, or a pencil skirt.

3. I believe a gorgeous suspender belt-and-stockings set is a work necessity. There is no better way to look polished, professional, and keep your stems covered during the winter. Added bonus: You feel lovely beneath your layers!

All-time favorite brands for office-appropriate bras?

The French really do know best when it comes to lingerie. Chantelle and Simone Perele make incredible bras for just about every size and style preference. Natori Feathers, a subtly sexy t-shirt bra, is one of our best-selling bras of all time. And for young professionals looking for function and fashion, Stella McCartney and Elle Macpherson Intimates are go-to brands.

The all-important bag question.

Handbags are often touted as the most important style statement you can make. Perhaps, but beware the it-bag. No matter how much you spend, it will still be "over" in six months.

Particularly when you're just beginning to build your wardrobe, you should choose a bag that's well-made, versatile, and can actually hold all your stuff. Opt for solid, neutral colors, and keep flashy branding to a minimum.

IF YOU JUST GRADUATED, YOU NEED...

A well-made, simple tote. (We like Cuyana, and
the large Le Pliage tote from Longchamp is a classic.)

IN A FEW YEARS, UPGRADE TO...

A polished, elegant carryall. (We have a thing
for Mansur Gavriel's large leather tote.)

ONCE YOU ARE MAKING BANK, GO FOR...

A head-turning handbag. (Céline, Louis Vuitton,
and Maiyet always look spot-on.)

ON
THE JOB

*In which you'll learn to avoid faux pas
and look amazing every day.*

Once you're actually working, you'll learn a ton by observing how your coworkers, superiors, and clients dress. There are examples of what to do (and what not to do!) all around you. Take mental notes, and don't be afraid to ask others about their style tricks and tips.

When it comes to looking sharp and setting yourself up for success, we swear by the following rules. Forgive us if some of them seem obvious, but we can all use a little reminder once in a while.

Avoid these common faux pas:

CLOTHES

Too-low neckline. If you're bordering on cleavage, retreat and reassess.

Too-short skirt. It may sound old-school, but the corporate world looks down on skirts that hit much above the knee.

Visible bra straps. Some things—like the color of your lingerie—should remain a mystery to your coworkers.

Pilling knitwear. A sweater comb will do wonders to bring your worn-in cardigan back to life. (The Laundress has a good one.)

Heels over four inches. If you're teetering or can't walk by the end of the day, they're too high.

Shirts with slogans or words. Your outfit should make a subtle statement—not a literal one.

Runway trends like thigh-high boots. We think they're cool, but your super-corporate clients probably won't.

Banged-up shoes. Shoe shining is not just for the gents. Get your heels shined, polished, and re-soled when necessary.

Woven friendship bracelets. Great for summer camp. Bad for corporate life.

BEAUTY / GROOMING

Chipped manicure. Nothing screams unprofessional like a two-week-old manicure. As soon as it starts to chip, remove it. Clean, bare nails are perfectly fine if you don't want to bother with nail polish.

Too much makeup. The more formal your work environment, the more natural your makeup should be.

No makeup. Even if you keep it minimal (a slick of mascara, a hint of lip color), a bit of makeup shows that you're making an effort.

Wet hair. Get a blow-dryer or shower at night, but don't show up to the office looking like you just got caught in a downpour (unless you did, in which case, you're excused).

Too-cute hairstyles. Pigtails have no place in a formal environment.

Ticketing bracelets or entry stamps. Your coworkers want to hear how awesome the music festival was, not see evidence of it. Grab a loofah and scrub that ink off before you leave for work.

Commit these faux pas and you'll not only look unprofessional, but you'll probably feel uncomfortable. Discomfort leads to distraction, and you can't build your empire when you're distracted.

A good rule of thumb: Once you put your clothes on in the morning, you shouldn't need to adjust them or think about them for the rest of the day.

Time to play.

Once you've been at your job for a few months, you'll naturally get a feel for both the explicit and implicit dress code of your office. Take cues from your coworkers about when you can get creative, and when you should keep it conservative. Observe for a few weeks before you decide how daring you want to get with:

× Nail color
× Statement jewelry
× Flats
× Open sandals
× Boots
× Loud prints / bright color
× Lip color

12 things to have on hand.

Murphy's Law applies to the office environment, too. Given the elements you might be up against (unexpected downpours, ice-cold air-conditioning, exploding ink cartridges, last-minute meetings), it's best to be prepared for anything and everything.

Keep the following items in your desk:

× Travel umbrella that can fit in a bag
× "Desk sweater" that lives on the back of your chair
× Thread and needle
× Stain remover pen (try Tide To Go)
× Lip balm
× Concealer and powder
× Tampons
× Band-aids
× Deodorant
× Dental floss
× Hairspray (for static cling)
× Pen and notebook

Bonus!
Two things to always have at home:

1. Iron / ironing board

It's important to have an iron for major wrinkle situations or to create neat creases in pants and shirts.

×   Our pick: Black & Decker

2. Handheld steamer

Perfect for quickly eliminating wrinkles from silks and lighter fabrics.

×   Our pick: Steamfast or Jiffy

A FIRST JOB CHECKLIST

*In which you'll ensure that your
look is on point before you get to work.*

Starting your first job? Go you.

The run-up can be a little nerve-wracking, so you'd best keep busy. Channel your energy into making sure your closet is equipped for your first few months. Beyond that, it's all about observing those around you and slowly building a wardrobe that will work for you.

One month out:

× Get in touch with your company's HR department to get the lowdown on the dress code. Don't be afraid to ask specific questions: Are heels the norm for women? Can you go sleeveless in the office? Do you have "casual Fridays," and do people *actually* go casual?

× Take stock of what's currently in your closet. Create a list of the items that are office-appropriate.

× Create "work" versus "play" sections in your closet.

× Buy an iron and a steamer.

Three weeks out:

× Come up with a vision for how you want to dress. It's mood board time!

× Based on this vision, buy your first few staples—enough to create five outfits. (Ultimately, you'll work your way up to your *Perfect Ten.*)

× Assess whether any items (old or new) need tailoring, and take them in for alterations.

Two weeks out:

× Buy some versatile accessories (shoes, knits, scarves, jewelry) that you can use to spice up the staples you've already bought.

× Spend a few full days in your new shoes to break them in and make sure you can comfortably get through the day.

× Shop for a basic handbag or tote that fits whatever you'll need at work (a laptop, a notebook, a tablet).

One week out:

× Try on your outfit for Day 1 to make sure it fits, feels good, and is clean and wrinkle-free. Wear it with the underwear you plan to wear, and check for visible bra straps or VPL.

× If problems arise, buy seamless underwear and a t-shirt bra that's undetectable under your clothes.

One day out:

× Lay out or hang up your outfit for Day 1. Iron or steam as necessary.

× Plan your outfits for Days 2-5. The first week at a new job can be exhausting, so do your styling ahead of time.

Three months in:

× Now that you've had time to soak up the office atmosphere, fill in holes in your wardrobe. Can you get a bit bolder with accessories? Do you need a suit?

× Shop for two or three new outfits to add to your rotation.

Six months in:

× Buy two or three additional outfits. Voilà! Your ten-outfit wardrobe is complete.

From here on out:

× Now that you've got the foundation of your wardrobe, start to experiment with statement pieces like a pair of graphic heels, a beautifully tailored coat, or a silk blouse in a bright color.

Damn, you look good.

That wasn't so hard, was it? When all is said and done, outfitting yourself in the morning should feel fun, easy, and even a bit indulgent. Pour some coffee, blast some music, and psych yourself up for the day ahead. You can't always control what's coming your way, but you can control how you look and feel as you face whatever pops up.

As legendary fashion editor Diana Vreeland suggested: Ultimately, it's never just about the dress. That said, creating a wardrobe you love is an important part of going after the career you want. So whether you love your current job or have your sights set on bigger and better things, never underestimate the importance of a power wardrobe.

And more importantly, never underestimate the woman who's wearing it (that would be you).

On that note, enough about clothes.

We know you have *#BetterThingsToDo.*

If you need us, we're at
mmlafleur.com

About the Authors

Sarah LaFleur

A Tokyo native and Harvard College graduate, Sarah LaFleur is the founder and CEO of MM.LaFleur, an NYC-based professional womenswear company. As a former management consultant, she knows all too well what it's like to gaze into a closet full of *blah*-feeling pantsuits. But these days, you'll find her happily rocking the MM.LaFleur uniform: dresses, dresses, and more dresses.

Tory Hoen

Tory is the Creative Director of Brand at MM.LaFleur. A graduate of Brown University and a former Paris resident, she has written and edited for outlets including *Fortune*, *New York Magazine*, *Time Out New York*, *Condé Nast Traveler*, and *Bon Appétit*. After years spent working in her freelancer uniform (pajamas), she now cleans up quite nicely for the office.

Photography:
Takahiro Ogawa
Lauren Coleman

Graphic Design:
be-pôles